Table of Contents

Super Mario Maker – Tips, Tricks, and Secrets

By Lantern Books

Super Mario Maker – Tips, Tricks, and Secrets is an unofficial Super Mario Guide guide. It is not associated with, approved, or endorsed by Super Mario Maker OR Nintendo. Super Mario Maker is the official trademark of Nintendo.

Use All The SPACE!

You can use up a TON of empty space all around your map by building doors that take players to some empty region. Areas that you would normally never be able to get to. This way you can make levels much longer!

It works like this: imagine that the top right part of your map is empty, just sky, somewhere along your map you can add a door way that takes the player to the top right of your map.

Here you can have them do whatever you'd like, use up the space as best as you can, and them send them back to the main level with another door way!

Don't Wait Nine Whole Days!

Do you want to use everything Super Mario Maker has to offer right now? Instead of waiting a whole 9 days for everything to slowly unlock?

Well all you need to do is place each of the items that arrive in every shipment into a new level just once. From there the next shipment should arrive in around 3 minutes. You just have to place all the items from the new shipment and repeat! You should have all the items in no time flat.

Jump Around

You can create some pretty cool level pieces by focusing just on the wall jump mechanic. There are a ton of different possibilities here that can add a bit of extra fun or that needed difficulty to your level. See what you can come up with using only the wall jump mechanic, it might just be that unique piece you need to have your level stand out online.

Draw a New Hand

You can switch up your hand type by tapping on the thumb stick, go left or right to swap through all your options. You can switch to a right hand or to a left hand. You can even pick out a variety of different skins for your hand such as colors and animal fur! Explore all the options to find the one you like the most.

Costume Party

If you finish the Mario 10 or Mario 100 challenge while wearing on of the character costumes, you can actually get an entirely different response from the Princess or the toad. See if you can trigger all the different combinations for the ultimate completion challenge.

Start with the Frame

Things can get messy quickly when you are building your level and you start placing items, enemies, and more all over the place. It can be hard to figure out where to go next, or what you want your overall level to look like. Instead start by focusing on the framework of your level first, just the barebones path that you want your level to look like.

Once you've got that frame in place and it plays well you can go crazy with the enemies, items, and more! The best part is that it's easy to change anything around in your framework to work with your enemies. The opposite is never as easy.

Get Those Doors In

You can use up to 4 doors each level. You can do a ton of cool stuff with that so be sure to use them all if you want to create massive and practically never ending levels!

Speed Things Up

You can save a huge amount of time and drastically speed up your level creation skills by using the huge amount of short cuts in the game! Check out the menu in game for some great time saving short cuts. Here are some useful ones to get you started:

Use the shoulder buttons and triggers to quickly copy and paste items, objects, or even entire sections of your level. You can get passed those long tedious sections of nothing but placing down items using these!

Start Strong

You can only upload 10 levels online when you first get started with the game. So make sure you upload your absolute best! That way you are much more likely to get some good star rating and have your upload limit raised.

You can make sure whatever you upload is good by creating a number of levels (anywhere from 3-10 is good) before you upload your first level. You can also ask your friends and family for their opinions about which one of your levels is their favorite.

Old Fashioned TV

You can change your game into the old fashioned 8-bit CRT TV during any loading screen! All you need to do is hold A and B while pressing down on the D-pad. Give it a shot and see what happens to your game!

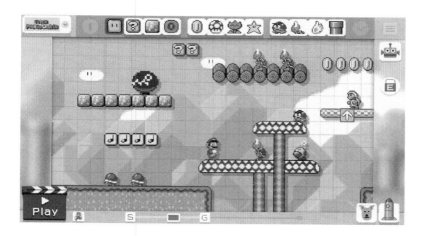

Wacky Yet Fun

There is a strong temptation to make your levels as wacky and crazy as possible by doing things like adding way too many enemies to an area or dropping in items that make the game a piece of cake. Try to balance the wacky elements in your level so the game is still challenging, rewarding, and above all fun.

Mario Amiibo

You can also get the old fashioned TV screen to activate by using the 30th anniversary Mario Amiibo. This will also spawn a giant mushroom for you! Check it out and see just what it can do.

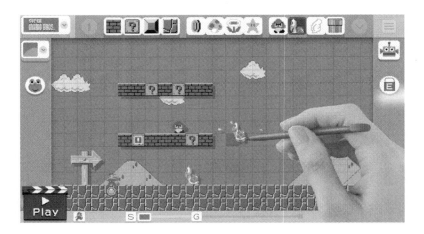

Even More Space!

You can use pipes to send players to the underground sections of your level. Be sure to use these pipes to add some serious variety to your levels and as an easy way to make your levels more challenging and if you want a bit longer.

Theme Party

If you want your level to stand out from the crowd, try creating each and every one of your levels with a theme in mind! Try focusing on things like a specific enemy type, certain items, even the specific moves or mechanics needed to finish the level. You can create a theme out of almost everything. If you do it right your level will automatically stand out from the rest!

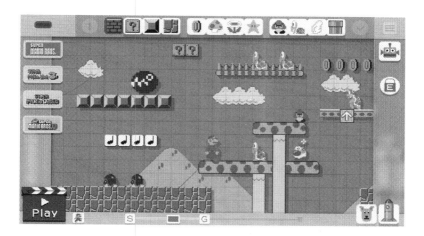

Suspense and Relax

A great way to build out your levels is by focusing on switching back and forth between suspenseful and tough sections followed by relaxing easy areas. Then repeat the process back and forth for the rest of your level. The constant back and forth will create an amazing level where the player can never know what to expect next, when done right there is a real sense of anticipation.

Focus!

Try to build out your level one bit at a time. If you jump around too much you risk forgetting what you wanted to build next and worse yet you might completely forget and miss entire sections, you wanted to build. At the very least write down what you were going to build before jumping ahead!

Be Nice and Help!

You can help out other level creators like yourself by playing their levels and leaving useful comments on parts that you liked and what you think could be improved upon. Be sure to leave enough detail to really help. And make sure to be friendly!

You'll be surprised by just how much you can learn by helping others improve their levels. You'll pick up on things you never even noticed before. You might even stumble upon something that can help you with your own levels.

Shake Shake Shake!

Every object that you can place down in the game will react different when you shake them! Give it a try and you might just be surprised or delighted by the results! Enemies react especially well!

Puzzle Builder

Making puzzles can be very difficult but it's an amazing feeling when you pull one off! The best thing you can do is keep trying. All great puzzles start off simple and though trial and error (and plenty of time) can become great and maybe even amazing.

Name of the Game

Always remember to keep in mind which Super Mario game you are working with. Each version of the game will play slightly differently with special items only working in one version or the other. In fact, you can use this to your advantage by creating a game in a specific style emulating one of the versions you are working with.

Better or Bigger

While making your maps bigger can make them more fun and make that fun last much longer sometimes it's a good idea to use things like doors and pipes to add alternate and different paths through your level. That way the player can pick and choose how they work through your level, and each player can play your level the way they like playing the game.

Titles of Fun

You can actually play around with the title screen of the game. Just grab your controller and start messing around. You can play around with (and mess up) things like the letters, spawn enemies, and even trigger unique sounds. See what else you can find out.

Just Get Going

The toughest and most intimidating part of any level is when you are just starting out and are straight out into an empty canvas (unless you already have an idea). The best thing you can do when you don't really know how to go is just to start building.

Don't load yourself down with thoughts of the long level ahead, instead just start placing bricks. At some point inspiration will strike and before you know it an amazing level will have appeared in front of you.

Star! Star! Star!

If you played someone else's level and you really liked what they created be sure to leave behind a star! That way they know someone played and liked their level. It will also let them upload more fun levels by increasing their upload limit.

Complex Down to Simple

You can usually break down complex level design to something much more simple without removing the difficulty and the fun. By doing this your levels will look and feel much more clean. They might even become a bit better for it. Whenever you think what you just built was too complicated try to figure out how you can make it just a bit simpler.

Erase vs Undo Dog

It's tempting to use erase for fixing mistakes and getting rid of anything you don't really want. But often it's not the right tool for the job. Using undo when you want to fix those little mistakes or start over on a particular part of your level is much faster!

It also doesn't risk you accidently deleting part of your level that you do want. Use the erase tool when you want to get rid of or replace entire massive sections of your level.

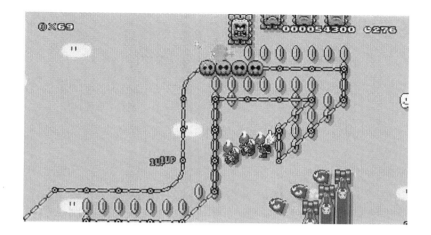

Tests for All

Before you upload your latest and greatest level, try having some of your friends or family (or both!) play your level. Watch how they do and how they play. You might just be surprised when they play the level in some way that you didn't suspect.

Maybe they get stuck on something you didn't intend. Or maybe your big challenge is actually one jump too easy. Use what you learn and what they say to make your level even better before unleashing it on the online community.

Pave with Gold

You can lead the player where you want them to go by using gold coins as a powerful reward. Simply place the gold coins along the path you want players to follow.

You can use this to create the obvious path or you can create a parallel second path that is tougher but has all the coins! You can also lead players away from the main path and send the to secret areas of your level just by placing gold coins along the way. See what other cool things you can come up with by leading the player through your levels.

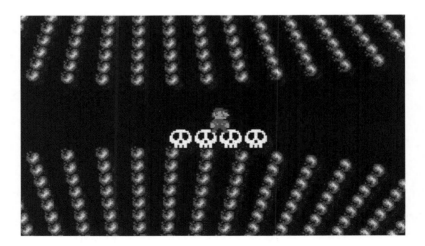

Read Thy Manual

The manual that comes with Super Mario Maker is not your standard black and white legal-speak filled manual. Instead is bursting with color, imagination, humor, and above all great advice. Check it out if you haven't already it's a great way to learn some cool tips from the creators of the game themselves! You won't regret it.

Unbeatable Pain

Make sure you can actually get past that difficult part in your level that you are building! You will have to play though the entire thing and beat it in order to actually post and share the level online! So don't spend too much time on something that might end up being literally impossible.

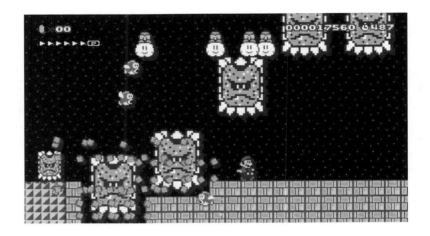

Comments!

Check out if any other players have left comments for you on your level online, there might be some useful feedback or a cool suggestion. They might even have caught a mistake that you made or something that is out of place. Either way it never hurts to check!

Buzzing Around

If you ever notice three flies buzzing around your screen swat them all to trigger a fun and exciting mini game! See if you can swat all the flies in the quick and fast paced game. It's an easy and fun way to take a quick break from creating your level for some quick action.

New and Exciting

Always be trying new ideas. Experimenting with unique and different level designs can make a drastic impact on how fresh and original your levels feel. Experimenting can also let you uncover exciting new ways to create levels. Who knows maybe one of your experiments could create the next big Super Mario Maker mechanic!

Keep Them Coming Back

If you happen to create crazy long levels be sure to make replaying them fun. Even the best map can get boring quickly if you have to play it over and over again. So make sure to place things like power ups such as super mushrooms and other fun items around your level! That way even the longest levels can stay interesting and fresh.

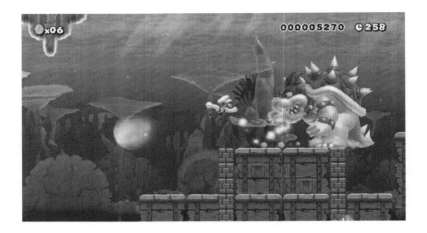

Pick Up Tricks

You can pick up a good number of tricks and tips from the Mario 10 challenge. Be sure to focus on how they use certain items or blocks and how that affects the level. You can also pay attention to how the entire level plays out, how they create the path the player walks through.

Once you've done this for a while you can bring those cool and unique ideas back to your own level and use them to build an even better level.

Old Fashion Inspiration

If you want to get some truly amazing inspiration for your new levels go back and play some of the old and original Mario games! If you inspect the levels and see how they are built you can copy or borrow some of the ideas and build one amazing level! You can even try creating tribute levels by creating an exact copy of your favorite levels.

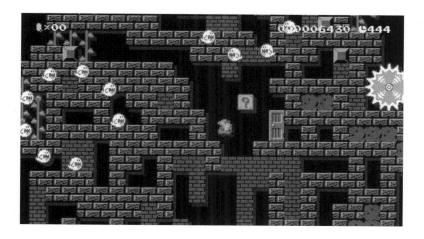

Thanks for reading! If you enjoyed this guide check out Lantern Books on Amazon. Here are some of our other guides that you might want to check out:

Disney Infinity 3.0: Tips, Tricks, and Secrets!

Disney Infinity: 3.0 - Tips, Tricks, and Secrets brings you the latest tips, tricks, and secrets that will take your gameplay to the next level! Discover all the hidden Easter eggs and hidden secret areas that Disney Infinity 3.0 has to offer!

Everything you learn in this guide will help you discover a whole new world inside of Disney Infinity 3.0. You will be able to explore new areas and use new abilities in a whole new light. Show off your new found knowledge of the game and its secrets to your friends! Get Disney Infinity: 3.0 - Tips, Tricks, and Secrets now.

Disney Infinity: 3.0 Character Guide

This is the best way to learn about all the different characters that Disney Infinity: 3.0 has to offer! You'll learn about over 20 different characters from all the Star Wars packs as well as characters like Joy and Sadness from Pixar's movie Inside Out, and characters like Olaf from frozen!

Discover all your favourite Disney characters in the Disney Infinity: 3.0 - Character guide, the must have companion to the game! If you want to learn about the strengths and weaknesses and see the amazing character figurines check this guide out now!

Printed in Great Britain
by Amazon.co.uk, Ltd.,
Marston Gate.